C000255388

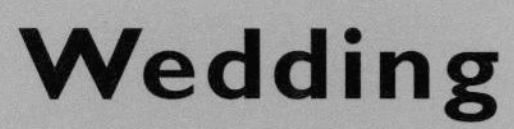
Wedding

Wedding Dresses

How to find your perfect wedding dress

from confetti.co.uk
don't get married without us...

First published in 2004
by Octopus Publishing Group
2–4 Heron Quays
London E14 4JP
www.conran-octopus.co.uk

A catalogue record for this book is available from the British Library.
ISBN 1 84091 366 5

Publishing Director Lorraine Dickey
Senior Editor Katey Day
Assistant Editor Sybella Marlow
Art Director Chi Lam
Designer Victoria Burley
Assistant Production Controller Natalie Moore

Other books in this series include *The Bride's Wedding*; *The Groom's Wedding*; *Your Daughter's Wedding*; *The Father of the Bride's Wedding; Men at Weddings; Wedding Readings & Vows*; *Getting Married Abroad*; *Wedding Speeches*; *Wedding & Special Occasion Stationery* and *The Wedding Book of Calm.*

Contents

Every bride knows the thrill of the feeling when she's found 'The One' – the one she will walk down the aisle with, enjoy the best day of her life with and dance the night away with. The one with whom she will experience that feeling of not wanting to go to sleep because it means having to close her eyes and stop looking at The One. Yes, the dress is a truly important part of any bride's wedding day.

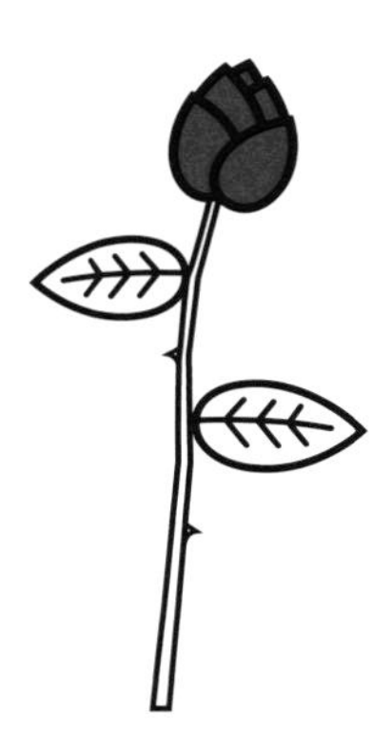

The One is different for every bride – ball gown, minidress, smart suit, trouser suit, slip dress, simple dress, fancy dress, jacket and dress, tiara, veil, big hat, feathers, no hat, rosebuds, high-heeled shoes, smart shoes, flip-flops, full-length gloves, or even a bikini.

When you're wearing The One, there's no need to ask whether you look good in it. You look fantastic, and you know you do.

A brief history

Early brides

Virginal white, or a shade thereof, is generally thought of as the traditional colour of wedding dresses in the UK. Brides in Ancient Egypt, Rome and Greece all wore dresses in various shades of white, but for most of the last 2,000 years brides have, in fact, worn all kinds of colours on their wedding day. Often they simply wore their best dress, or sometimes a new one, to get married. This was very convenient, as at least they could wear it again afterwards.

Queen Victoria & royal weddings

Queen Victoria is usually credited with the popularization of the white wedding dress – even though her dress wasn't actually white at all. Her dress for her wedding on 10 February 1840 composed of a bodice and skirt of plain cream silk satin, with a spectacular lace veil and skirt flounce. Cream was already quite a popular choice for wedding gowns at this time, but there is no doubt that Victoria's endorsement of the colour helped to establish it. She certainly set a royal trend, as subsequent British queens have all worn cream dresses at their weddings (incorporating Victoria's antique Honiton lace into their dresses as something borrowed!).

Although each royal wedding dress spawned a host of imitations across the land, probably the most influential dress since Queen Victoria's was that worn by Lady Diana Spencer, whose 1981 wedding to Prince Charles set the style for the next 15 years. Her fairytale ball gown with huge ruched sleeves and a long train created a new concept in sheer extravagance and spectacle of a wedding dress.

Modern-day dresses

Mrs Wallis Simpson, a bride who married a former king, wore a very different outfit at her wedding to Edward VIII, in 1937. Her simple floor-length dress with matching jacket was specially designed for her in a colour created to match her eyes, dubbed 'Wallis Blue'. Complementing this she wore a pink and blue feathered hat. Contemporary reports suggest the outfit was much admired and imitated: it is said to be the single most copied dress in fashion, and certainly wedding, history.

The bridal fashions of each decade of the 20th century continue to influence and inspire modern brides. In the 21st century, high street fashions have had an effect on wedding wear – the asymmetrical look and diamanté fad are recent examples. Even 1980s dresses, with their fussy ruffles and flounces which used to be seen as the antithesis of all things contemporary, could be set for a comeback in the current '80s revival.

Choosing your dress

When you imagine your perfect wedding day, do you see a realistic image of yourself?

We all want to look our most gorgeous for the big day, but in reality we know that most of us don't look much like the celebrity icons of glossy magazines. Worried? Don't be. Beauty comes in all different shapes and sizes, and the surest way to look your best is to concentrate on the real image of yourself. Just aim to look like you – only even more fantastic.

When thinking about the image you want to create, think about what you normally wear, your favourite colours, where the ceremony's taking place, and the tone you're aiming for – relaxed, traditional or avant-garde. Once you have these elements in mind, you can apply them to your wedding outfit.

If your body or choice of ceremony isn't right for a white puffy dress, don't feel you have to go for it just because of the traditional image of a bride. It's usually a good idea to try a variety of different styles, even those you think you will hate, as you may be surprised with what suits you.

Dress styles

Ball gown

This is the ultimate 'Cinderella shall go to the ball!' dress. Ball gowns are the most traditional style of skirt for the bride who is after a classic look. The skirt's appearance may vary from structured and heavy-looking to soft and light, depending on the fabric used. This style of skirt is often combined with a fitted bodice with a natural or dropped waistline, and suits a wide range of figures, especially those with curves. These dresses are usually worn with a hooped underskirt, which may have to be bought separately, to keep the skirts plumped out and full.

Like most dress styles, the ball gown lends itself to being either a one-piece dress or a separate bodice and skirt.

There is a trick to walking in full skirts like this. You give the hoop a tiny little kick before taking a step, to move it out of the way and make sure you don't trip over it. Many a bride has looked unbelievably gracious floating down the aisle, all the while muttering 'kick, step, kick, step' to herself!

Classic ball gown wedding dresses:

Lady Diana Spencer
Victoria Beckham

Empire-line

The empire-line dress is for brides who don't want a figure-hugging gown. The skirt starts just below the bust and is not as full as in the ball gown or A-line shape. While this style of dress best suits a small-busted, slim figure, empire-line dresses are also a good choice for pregnant brides, as their lack of waist means there is no constriction, and they can be roomy.

When such dresses were in fashion in the early 19th century, they were worn with a small, neat bonnet, and a simple bag was carried, much like the small fabric bags currently in vogue. This look could make a wonderful alternative historical outfit.

Classic empire-line wedding dress:
Kate Winslet

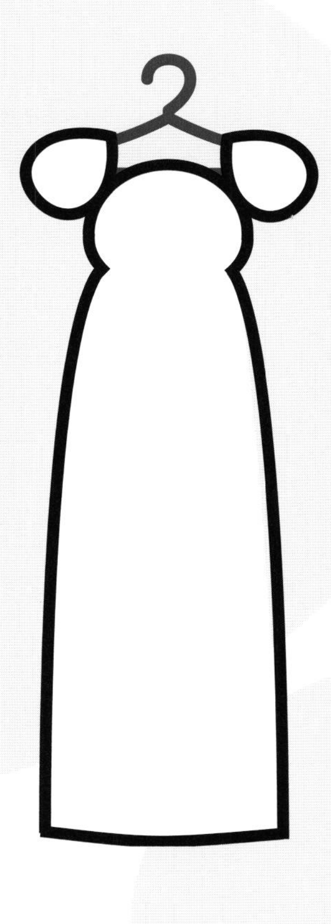

A-line

As the name suggests, A-line dresses are 'A-shaped', with vertical seams running from the waist or shoulders to the bottom of the skirt. The degree of flare in the skirt can vary from slight to extreme, and the bodice is often fitted. This style suits most people, and is indeed the most popular dress style at the beginning of the 21st century.

A-line dresses also make a great choice for separates. If you go with this option, instead of matching the top and bottom, why not go for a bit of drama or contrast? Try mixing colours, such as a red bodice with a gold skirt, or a baby-blue bodice and ivory skirt. You can also go for completely different fabrics for each item, making them easier to 'recycle' into your post-wedding wardrobe.

Heavier versions of this style will require the 'kick step' technique for walking, as described on page 14.

Classic A-line wedding dresses:

Gwen Stefani
Caroline Corr
Lisa Marie Presley

Column/straight

The column design is for brides who want a modern, chic look. The slim profile skims the body's curves and looks flattering on tall, slim or petite brides. It's also popular for simple weddings and register offices – but remember, just because the surroundings may be unassuming, that doesn't mean your dress has to be.

There are a number of ways to thrill in a column dress; a demure look from the front may be broken up by a backless style. You could opt for an asymmetric floral sash instead of sleeves, like Victoria Beckham's reception dress. Or, how about a daring split skirt or a dramatic overcoat? Straight styles are the easiest to pair with coats, cloaks and wraps.

Classic column wedding dresses:
Heather Mills
Sophie Rhys Jones

Mermaid

Similar to the column but even more figure-hugging, the mermaid style flares out at the bottom. This type of skirt is often bias-cut (that is cut on the diagonal), and is perfect for a bride wanting to accentuate her curvaceous figure.

Wearing a wedding dress is not about finding the dress that makes you look the thinnest or tallest, or whatever ideal of beauty you aspire to. It's about finding the dress that, in the words of the song, will 'accentuate the positive'. You want to find the dress that reflects you and your personality. Work on this, rather than worrying over those stubborn last few pounds!

Classic mermaid wedding dress:
Courtney Cox

Fishtail

The fishtail looks like a column or mermaid style from the front, but has an extra panel of fabric sewn into the back of the skirt that fans out to make a little train, earning the style its name. This dress style was first seen in the UK in the late 19th century, and has remained popular ever since for wedding dresses. This means that you can occasionally pick up a fantastic vintage piece and look totally modern but completely unique in it.

When buying a dress like this, make sure you can walk in it, especially if you normally like to take big strides. Another word of caution: people may accidentally stand on your little train. Always check before moving off!

Classic fishtail wedding dresses:

Kerry Katona
Ffion Hague

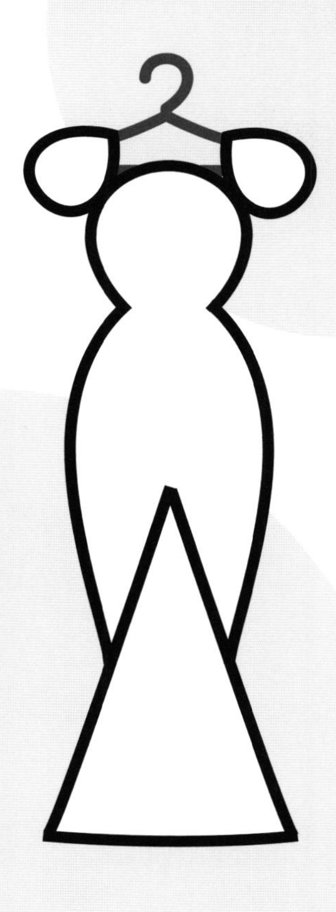

Slip dress

Although not strictly a dress style, more a version of the column dress, this is becoming so popular we think it worthy of inclusion here. Informal and beach weddings are on the rise, and many brides opt for a stylish slip in white or a pale colour, often with spaghetti straps (see page 38).

These dresses are very flattering to most shapes, provided that they are cut well. Many styles are cut on the bias to complement curves. Slip dresses are very versatile lengthwise. They can be worn as tiny mini or full length styles.

Classic slip wedding dresses:

Sarah Michelle Gellar
Carolyn Bessette Kennedy
Cindy Crawford

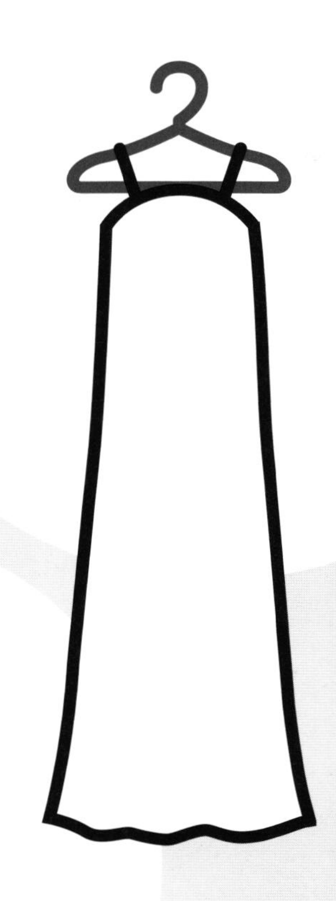

Trains

The train – the elongated section of material at the back of the bridal gown – can accompany any dress shape or style. It can vary in length from very short to very long, but most brides (royalty excluded) opt for a train no longer than 2.5m (8ft). Many prefer not to have one at all, but it is possible to have the best of both worlds by choosing a detachable train, usually attached to the dress at the waist by means of hooks or buttons.

If your train is not detachable, it should have hooks that you can use to loop it up to the waist (bustle-style) or shoulders. Some dresses adopt the old-fashioned but elegant style in which the loop is held over the fingers.

Much less common is the 'Watteau' train, which falls from the back, near the shoulders, to the floor. Usually detachable, these are more popular in the US than in the UK.

Duster train

The duster is the shortest train available, trailing no more than about 30cm (1ft) from the point at which the dress reaches the floor.

Chapel train

A medium-length train that is popular and manageable, extending 1–1.2m (3–4 ft) from the waist.

Cathedral train

A long, formal train stretching 1.8–2.2m (6–7 ft) from the waist. You may need the assistance of your bridesmaids and/or pageboys to hold the train at certain points during the day, in order to protect it from being damaged. A train any longer than this style is generally called a 'monarch' train.

Necklines

After the general profile of the dress, the second most important concern is usually the neckline. Most brides find themselves firmly one side or the other of the straps/strapless divide, but there are many further variations beyond this simple choice.

The neckline is important because it draws attention to the upper part of the body, especially the face, collarbones and *décolletage* (throat and cleavage). For this reason, getting a neckline exactly right for you is very important. Necklines also contribute to the overall style of the gown, and will affect what accessories you can (or can't) wear with it.

Scoop/round

The scoop is a U-shaped neckline, often cut quite low and echoed on the back of the dress. This is a style that suits any bride.

Halterneck

The halterneck features straps that join at the back of the neck, or a high neck with wide armholes. It usually has a very low-cut back, so is best worn without a bra. This style looks good on brides with great shoulders!

Crumbcatcher

The crumbcatcher is essentially a square neckline with a double fold of material, so that one layer projects slightly from the body.

Queen Anne

As the name suggests, this neckline recalls the style of dress worn during the reign of Queen Anne in 18th-century England. The design features a heart-shaped neckline in the front and a high back, which is often joined to the front by sleeves cover the shoulders or are full-length. This style is for brides who wish to display their cleavage with taste!

Sweetheart

The sweetheart is a low neckline, similar in shape to the Queen Anne but slightly less accentuated. The back is usually cut at a similar height to the front, but without the curvy heart shape.

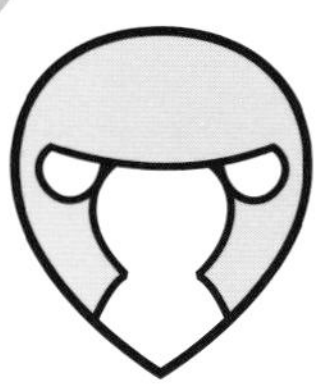

Off-the-shoulder

The broad, sweeping off-the-shoulder neckline features small sleeves or straps that sit just below the shoulder on the upper arm, showing off the shoulders and collarbone. It is good for curves and for medium- to full-chested brides, but not ideal for those with wide shoulders.

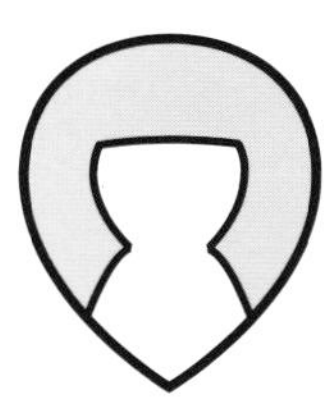

Strapless

The strapless bodice is usually figure-hugging, often with a straight or subtly-shaped neckline. This style is good for those with broad shoulders.

V-neck

The V-neck dips down to a V-shape at the front, which draws attention away from the bust line. The back may be similarly cut or else be higher and straighter. This style suits brides with a medium bust.

Square

The square neckline is cut straight across, with angled corners where the straps or sleeves meet the bodice. This is a style for almost any bride.

Boatneck

The wide shape of the boatneck follows the collarbones almost to the tips of the shoulders. The front and back panels are either joined at the extremities or separated by thin straps.

Jewel/T-shirt

The jewel neckline is round and high-cut, sitting near the base of the throat. This style is good for small-busted brides and those wishing to cover up their upper chest and collarbones.

Asymmetrical

This includes any neckline that is different on the left and right of the bodice. The dramatic example shown here is a one-shoulder design, perfect for the bride who doesn't need to wear a bra.

Shoelace/spaghetti strap

The neckline is usually straight or slightly shaped, and the bodice is supported by very thin, delicate straps, which are sometimes detachable. This style is good for small- to medium-chested brides.

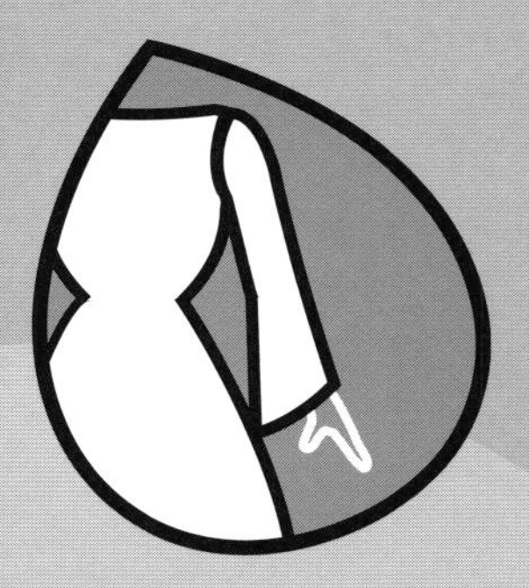

Sleeve lengths and styles

The decision whether or not to have sleeves used to be dictated by seasonal fashion, but now it is more a matter of personal taste. The type of sleeve you choose will be influenced by the overall style of the dress – and by how fond you are of your upper arms!

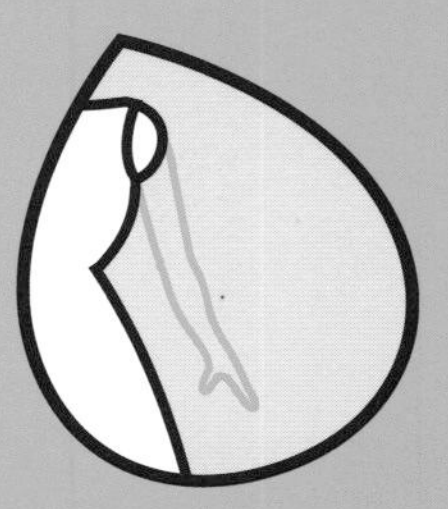

Cap

This is a very short sleeve just covering the shoulder, and therefore best suited to brides with slender or well-toned upper arms. It is usually combined with a scoop or boatneck.

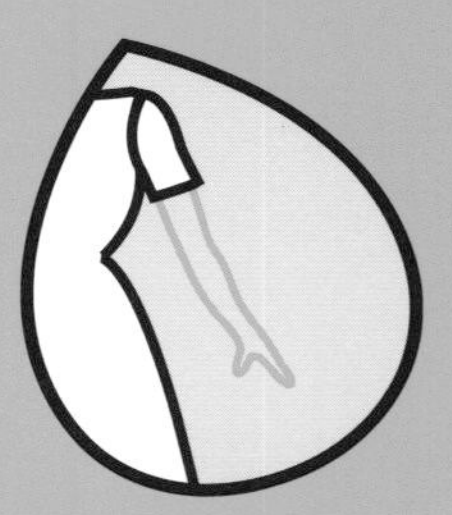

Short/T-shirt

Longer than the cap and extending to the middle of the upper arm, the short sleeve is perfect for brides who want to cover their upper arms. If you're worried about displaying your arms but have fallen in love with a short-sleeved style, add a bolero jacket or a wrap for a stylish cover-up.

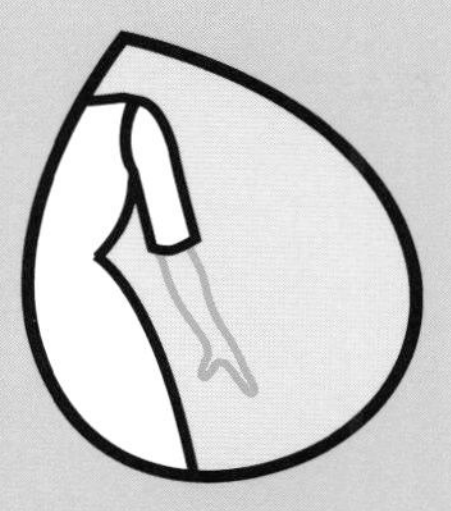

Elbow-length

As the name implies, this is a longer version of the short sleeve/T-shirt that reaches to the elbow. Avoid elbow-length sleeves if you have very short or broad arms, as they may look constricting.

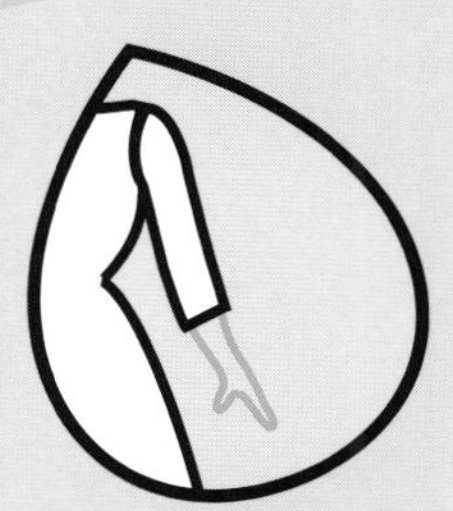

Three-quarter-length

The three-quarter-length sleeve, reaching the midpoint between elbow and wrist, is a style that is currently in vogue. This is a demure look that still allows you to wear a bracelet, or even a very delicate watch.

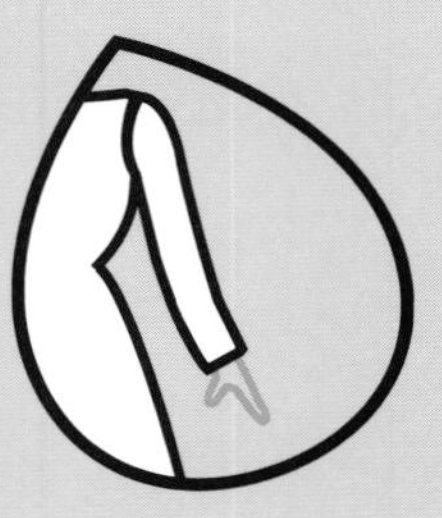

Long

The long sleeve is slender and runs from shoulder to wrist. Translucent sheer fabrics are a popular choice for this type of sleeve.

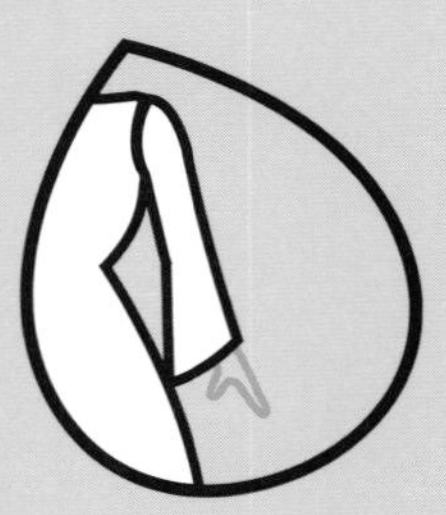

Bell-shaped

The bell-shaped sleeve is slender from the shoulder to elbow or mid-forearm, then flares out to the wrist. The sleeve is typically long, and sometimes has tails that extend beyond the fingertips.

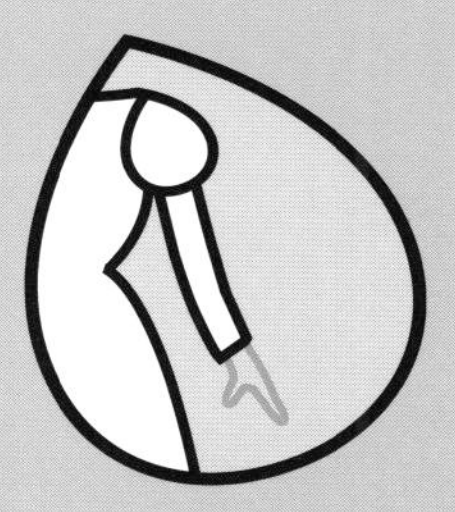

Juliet

This style of Shakespearean inspiration has a long fitted sleeve and puff shoulder, and looks fabulous on an empire-line or column dress.

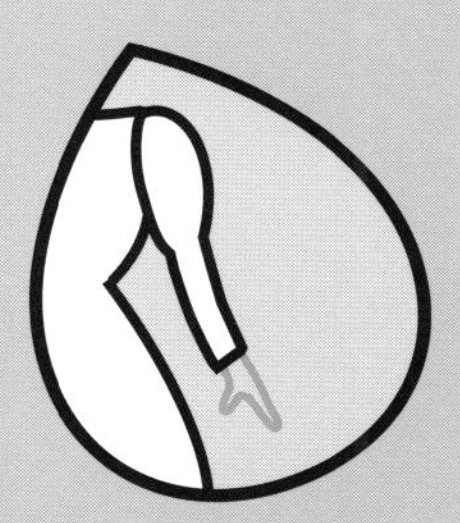

Balloon

The balloon sleeve – full over the upper arm down to the elbow, then slender from elbow to wrist – is a classic choice to accompany a big skirt!

Choosing the style that's right for you

If your shape tends to the tall and thin...

...you could choose a ball gown with a strapless, fitted bodice. However, if you feel your shoulders are too bony or that your collarbones protrude too much, go for a long fitted dress, perhaps with a high neckline. You may feel that you are too thin for this style, but your height and leanness could be beautifully set off by some lovely delicate detailed embroidery or beading.

If you are short with a fuller, feminine figure...

...try an empire-line dress. The beauty of this style is that it has a seam under the bust line and then just flows down. In the right fabric, the dress will not sit to your body, but will glide around it. Although a knee-length dress could also work for you, this longer shape will give you a nice tall silhouette.

Sleeves are an option, depending on how you feel about your arms. If you do opt for sleeves, go for long and narrow, and not too tight.

If your hair is piled high on your head, this will also give you more height, but do not go for this hairstyle if you have a round face.

If you have a very full bust...
...draw attention away from it by having a long bodice, such as a basque, and a full skirt. Dresses that use the natural waistline, by contrast, will draw attention to the bust area. Make sure your bodice area is very plain, and avoid low necklines. If you are really keen on detail, save it for the lower part of the skirt.

If you have full or wide hips...
...avoid a bustle, peplum or anything tiered. Most other styles of dress are just fine, but make sure you choose something that doesn't fit too tightly over the hip area. The A-line' style, which is fitted on top and then flares slightly to the hem, will disguise larger hips by creating a slight triangle on the lower half of your body. Even the ball gown look, in quite a simple material, will draw attention away from the hips. The empire line will work, too, if your bust is a bit smaller, but could end up downplaying your waist and stomach area.

If you have wide shoulders...
...consider narrowing your look with wide straps, or cover the shoulders completely and divert the focus to a V-neckline. It's important to show some skin around this area, but, if need be, you can soften the effect by wearing a sheer wrap around your shoulders. Make sure you stay away from puff sleeves!

If your legs are short or on the heavy side...
...it's a good idea to opt for a long dress. Give yourself more height with a column style, which is straight but not too body-hugging.

If your arms are on the short side...
...three-quarter-length sleeves will help to make them look longer. Whatever you do, don't go sleeveless.

If your arms are chubby...
...go for long simple sleeves that are not skin-tight.

You may feel that you aren't right for any style of dress, but just remember that you always find something to put on every other day you go out into the world. Some days you feel better than others – and those are the days when people pay you compliments. On your wedding day, you'll feel fantastic, and you'll earn all those compliments.

Above all, remember – it's not just about the dress – you also have a personality, an aura, vitality, a whole package to work with. People aren't going to be looking at a dress in isolation – they'll be looking at the whole you. And if you're happy about what you're doing, nothing could look more beautiful than that.

Choosing the perfect fabric

The fabric you choose will be dictated partly by the style of your dress. For instance, a stiff satin is more suitable for a ball gown silhouette than for an informal style, which would be much better suited to a floating chiffon.

Here are some of the main types of fabric and their qualities:

Chiffon

A delicate, matt fabric that drapes and skims. Feather-light and perfect for layering, sleeves and even veils, this fabric makes a beautiful complement to crêpes or satins in the same dress, or can be used for sheer wraps and scarves for brides and bridesmaids.

Crêpe, georgette and satin-backed crêpe

Crêpe is a softly flowing fabric with a crinkled texture, popular for both brides and bridesmaids. It works well on slim-shaped dresses that can be cut on the bias to create a flattering silhouette. Georgette (sometimes called georgette crêpe) is very similar. Satin-backed crêpe is reversible so that the satin side can be complemented by the matt crêpe side in the same dress, for instance in cuffs, borders, panels or the neckline.

Organza and silk organza

Similar to chiffon but stiffer, organza works well on shimmering skirts and ballet-dancer-style dresses for bridesmaids. Silk organza is often embroidered.

Shantung and raw silk

These are very popular textured silks, with natural imperfections and 'slubs', making each length unique. They are medium to heavy fabrics, and their natural texture makes them suitable for simple gowns.

Duchesse satin

This is what most people think of when they hear the words 'wedding dress material'! A rich, glossy satin with a matt back, this is a good fabric for embellishing with beads and jewels as it is relatively strong.

Taffeta and moiré

Taffeta is the classic formal party dress material, quite stiff and usually made from silk, although it can be synthetic. Moiré is taffeta with the classic 'watermark' look. Both fabrics are traditionally used for ball-gown-style dresses.

Brocade

Brocades have rich weaves with raised designs, in either the same or contrasting colours. Rich and magnificent brocades are perfect for heavier dresses with full skirts and trains, or for boned bodices. These fabrics are suitable for brides or perhaps matrons of honour, and cloaks and gowns with a historical theme.

Tulle/embroidered tulle

Tulle is essentially fine mesh netting – think tutus. Very light and usually worn in combination with other fabrics, it can complement crêpes or satins beautifully.

Velvet/devoré

A plush material with a plain underside, velvet is often used for cloaks and historically themed dresses. It is currently enjoying popularity in a patterned version, known as devoré, which is great for slip dresses.

Choosing the perfect colour for you

According to the old (and rather scary) rhyme, only blue and white will do for wedding dresses:

Married in white
You have chosen aright

Married in green
Ashamed to be seen

Married in grey
You'll go far away

Married in red
You'll wish yourself dead

Married in blue
Love ever true

Married in yellow
Ashamed of your fellow

Married in black
You'll wish yourself back

Married in pink
Your spirits will sink

For many women, coloured dresses make better options than white, as pure white is often draining to the complexion. Wedding gowns in cream, pale gold, pale blue and pink are all quite usual now, and there's recently been a move towards much deeper colours: shades of green or even burgundy – particularly stunning for a winter wedding.

In general, the paler your skin, the more suitable bright white will be for you. Those with yellower skin tones (usually redheads, strawberry blondes and those with freckles) will suit ivories and creams. Darker skins should avoid stark whites, and English roses (with pink undertones) should go for off-whites.

According to another popular old rhyme, brides should incorporate 'something old, something new, something borrowed and something blue' into their outfit. It's not uncommon for brides to sew a small blue ribbon into the inside hem of their dress for luck.

Advice for larger brides

If your figure is on the generous side, buying clothes can be a nightmare. Every woman over a size 14 has tales to tell of trying to squeeze into something too small in full, embarrassing view of a communal changing room packed with size 8 skinnies, or of shops simply not stocking clothes in their size at all. So the thought of buying a wedding dress fills many bigger women with dread. If finding ordinary, fun-to-wear clothes is humiliating, if not impossible, buying the dress of your dreams is bound to be even more of an ordeal – isn't it?

Good news, bad news

The good news is that, when it comes to wedding dresses, a wider variety of larger sizes is available than you'd find in ordinary trendy gear. Manufacturers seem to feel (mistakenly) that curvier women can do without a pair of jeans or a sparkly top, but that girls of all shapes and sizes need wedding dresses.

The bad news is that, because of limited space, bridal shops don't usually carry a full range of stock in every size. Instead, they carry samples on which orders are based, and these come in a limited range of sizes – sometimes stopping at size 12! This means that, even though you can order a dress in a larger size, if you can't fit into the sample in stock, it's impossible to tell exactly how that style will look on you. For some, this turns the search for their dream dress into a thoroughly depressing experience.

However, being curvaceous doesn't mean you can't get the dress of your dreams – and look fantastic in it, too.

See www.confetti.co.uk/fashion/features/larger_sizes.asp for details of companies and stores that can provide dresses in any size.

Planning ahead

To take the sting out of looking for a dress, do a bit of research beforehand. Call the stores in advance, find out exactly what is available to try on and whether they do alterations once the dress has been ordered. Remember that samples can act as rough guides – often stores have ways of fitting them around you so that you can get an idea of how the dress will look.

Knowing exactly what you want obviously helps when you are looking for a dress – if you're sure a particular style will suit you, you won't need to struggle into a sample, so take a good look around. You could try Confetti's dress search to get ideas. Start by thinking about what styles usually suit you and work from there. Keep an open mind and try on dresses at stores with larger sample sizes. After all, you don't have to buy everything you try on.

Style guide

There's no one style that suits any particular size – it all depends on your proportions. A completely straight dress is unlikely to be flattering if you are very curvy, but it would be more suitable if you're fortunate enough to have a very flat stomach. Avoid puffs and gathers, too. A-line dress styles always look good, and silks and satins are preferable to very body-hugging fabrics.

Fortunately, fashion is on your side. Contemporary lines are much cleaner, and basques, which give great waist definition, are very much in vogue.

If you do decide to do something radical about your weight before your wedding, remember two things. First, don't set too ambitious a target. If you're a size 18 and you buy a size 12 dress but only make it to size 14, you will have a very uncomfortable wedding day. Second, many brides lose some weight in the final weeks before the wedding, mainly through nerves and manic rushing around! So, while you shouldn't count on this to get into your dress, you may want to make allowances for it when having your fittings.

Pregnant and looking for a dress?

You're not alone. One London wedding dress store recently estimated that up to 20 per cent of its customers were expecting, and pregnancy has never been bigger on the star circuit, with celebrities from Madonna to Catherine Zeta Jones showing off their fecund tummies with pride.

But all this doesn't mean that the idea of doing the big day with a bump isn't daunting for brides, especially when it comes to choosing the dress. The social stigma may be all but gone, but pregnancy chic hasn't quite penetrated the wedding arena: few of the major stores carry specific maternity lines, leaving many brides-to-be in fear that they won't be able to find anything to flatter their burgeoning figures. However, although they may not advertise the fact, wedding dress suppliers do stress that they will try to ensure that the pregnant bride won't miss out on the dress of her dreams.

Planning ahead

When it comes to the dress, bump doesn't have to equal frump. On the other hand, any pregnant bride has to take certain things into account. The big day will be a long day, and if you're expecting (or if you've just had a baby), you're bound to get tired more easily than usual. This means that comfort has to be paramount in your choice of what to wear. Don't try to force yourself into a corset: you'll only faint. Be honest with the person who is providing the dress. If you are pregnant, tell them – even if you don't want anyone else to know.

The dress will have to accommodate a pregnant bride's changing shape, too. Look for a supplier who's prepared to be flexible and carry out alterations as close to the wedding as possible.

If you can afford it, try to find a designer who will make the dress individually and leave the alterations until as late as possible. Changes in bust size will also affect pregnant brides-to-be and breastfeeding mothers: like all future brides, you should go to fittings wearing the same bra as the one you intend to wear on the big day.

Pregnant fashion no-nos

Of course you don't need to sacrifice style for the sake of comfort but, for most pregnant women, clinched waists, very tight-fitting dresses and the currently fashionable tight-laced bodices will be out. Instead, why not show off your new curves with a focus on the shoulders and bust? If you want to show off your bump, it may be worth talking over a style with an individual designer. Stretchy, jersey-type material is already proving popular with some American brides and mums-to-be.

Empire-line or A-line dresses are all perfect for pregnant brides. In all these styles, the dress flares from under the bust, although the empire line has a straighter skirt.
You could also add a chiffon overdress to complete the outfit. Or you could plump for a medieval-style dress with long, flowing sleeves. Don't feel shy about wearing white, traditionally a symbol of 'purity', as this is no longer taboo.

Weddings abroad

What you wear for a wedding abroad will be very much dictated by the climate. A full ball gown with tight bodice lacings may be something of a health hazard under a tropical sun, while a faux fur cloak may be only just enough to keep you warm in Lapland! Even once you've decided on your location, there may be different options available – for instance, a Caribbean resort might offer a beach, hotel or lawn ceremony, which could also influence your decision.

Generally, the greatest concern of brides marrying abroad is how to transport the dress. A full service airline, given enough warning, is usually able to accommodate the dress in the cabin, but always check first – nothing is more likely to cause chaos than assuming this, only to find out that for some reason the dress has to go in the hold. If you don't have a special dress bag, you can cover the dress in a duvet cover and then a suit cover (if you have one large enough!).

If you marry abroad using a package holiday firm, they will make provision in their planes for the safe transport of your dress. Check with them for full information on their recommended procedure.

Read *Getting Married Abroad*, also in this series, for more advice and ideas.

Wearing the trousers

Ever since Bianca Jagger married in that white Yves St Laurent suit (with quite clearly nothing on underneath), trousers have been an acceptable – if still daring and different – option. A word of warning, however: if you are marrying in church, you should be attired fittingly for the solemnity of the occasion. Check with your vicar how he feels about plunging necklines and hipster trousers before you stride gaily down the aisle.

Many brides choose smart suits with skirts or trousers for their wedding outfit. This is when hats, a wedding staple, really come into their own. If you can afford it, treat yourself here – a hat by a top milliner is the kind of thing every girl should have once in her life!

Historical/themed dresses

A number of top designers concentrate on historical dresses. The most popular are undoubtedly medieval-style gowns, but 1920s and 1930s styles are also sought after.

If you're on a tight budget, try internet auction sites as these are a great place to find vintage dresses.

Your dress and your bouquet

As well as the colour of your flowers, the shape of your bouquet should depend on the style of your dress and overall theme of your wedding. As a rule, try to create a contrast – unless you truly believe more is more. If you are marrying in a full-skirted dress, a posy-style bouquet is best. A column dress, on the other hand, is complemented by a shower bouquet (which has a lot of horizontal lines). These are often composed of lilies or orchids, which themselves echo the simplicity of the dress. Short dresses and dresses with full skirts will always look better with a fuller, rounder posy-style bouquet. The traditional advice is to avoid cascading waterfall bouquets with a cascading skirt!

Hold the bouquet approximately in front of your tummy button to display it to best effect with your dress.

Designer Advice: Stewart Parvin

Stewart Parvin has been creating elegant and classic clothing since 1986. He began designing bridal wear in response to the demand from his couture clients, and now he has his own boutique, Stewart Parvin Couture, based in London. He designs a couture collection, as well as individual creations, and can boast celebrities and royalty among his clients.

Q. What are the three most important things for a bride to consider when choosing her dress?

A. (i) Budget.
(ii) The type of wedding – it's important to wear a dress that is appropriate for the ceremony and venue.
(iii) Body shape – find a dress that flatters her best point and hides her worst!

Q. What is the biggest mistake a bride can make with her dress?

A. Hugely overspending, and regretting it.

Q. What's the best piece of advice you can offer a bride about her dress?

A. Relax – it's a dress, not a matter of life and death! Enjoy it, and don't stress.

Designer Advice: Suzanne Ermann

Suzanne Ermann trained and opened her first workshop in Paris designing evening dresses. She started designing a line of wedding dresses because she wanted to make them fashionable and fresh. Her reputation grew, and her designs are now distributed around the world. Suzanne's signature design includes hoops and swirls, in a range of fabrics and materials.

Q. What are the three most important things for a bride to consider when choosing her dress?

A. (i) Shape.
(ii) Fabric.
(iii) Style.

Q. What is the biggest mistake a bride can make with her dress?

A. Not feeling like herself when she wears the dress.

Q. What's the best piece of advice you can offer a bride about her dress?

A. To pick a dress that not only flatters her shape and makes her feel beautiful, but one that also expresses her personality.

Designer Advice: Ian Stuart

Ian Stuart studied Bridal and Evening Wear Design at university in Britain before moving to New York, and is one of the hottest young designers around. Having won 'New Designer of the Year' at the 1999 British Bridal Awards, his own label has attracted worldwide acclaim. The Ian Stuart International Collection displays the cutting-edge, sexy end of bridal wear, with his trademark of customizing each gown to the bride's own personality.

Q. What are the three most important things for a bride to consider when choosing her wedding dress?

A. (i) No one else should make the choice for her.
(ii) Her personality should show through.
(iii) It should come from a reputable bridal store.

Q. What is the biggest mistake a bride can make with her dress?

A. Leaving the purchase too late and not having enough time for alterations.

Q. What's the best piece of advice you can offer a bride about her dress?

A. Don't be too influenced by family and friends as it is your day, your wedding and your dress.

Designer Advice: Beverly Lister

Based in the UK, Beverly Lister has been designing for her own brand, Promise, since 1991. She calls the Promise style 'classic 50s, updated for today's bride'. Beverly previously designed evening wear for a famous fashion house.

Q. What are the three most important things for a bride to consider when choosing her wedding dress?

A. (i) It should flatter her shape
(ii) It should suit her personality
(iii) It has to make you feel gorgeous!

Q. What is the biggest mistake a bride can make with her dress?

A. Choosing a gown that doesn't reflect her personality.

Q. What's the best piece of advice you can offer a bride about her dress?

A. The most elegant brides look totally relaxed. Choose a gown that makes you feel gorgeous, but that you don't have to think about at all.

Designer Advice: Mirror Mirror Couture

Maria Yiannikaris and Jane Freshwater have been designing wedding gowns for 16 years, and are probably most famous for their creations for Amanda Holden and Zoë Ball. Before setting up their couture studio in north London, they worked in mainstream fashion.

Q. What are the three most important things for a bride to consider when choosing her wedding dress?

A. (i) Style and shape – it should flatter your body and sit well with your personality.

(ii) Colour or shade – very important, the right tone will make your skin glow!

(iii) Choose a reputable shop or designer that you feel confident with.

Q. What is the biggest mistake a bride can make with her dress?

A. To choose a less flattering shape simply because she likes the design.

Q. What would your advice be to a bride who fell in love with a dress that was out of her budget?

A. We would try to show some cost effective alternatives or suggest to have sparking wine instead of champagne – revise the guest list and have the dress!

Buying your dress

Now you've got a good grasp of the different styles and terminologies, where do you start looking for it?

The Internet – many designers have their own websites featuring some or all of their current collections. You can also find hundreds of dresses from a range of designers at www.confetti.co.uk/fashion/fashion_search/dress_search/default.asp

Magazines – general wedding magazines include a number of advertisements for dress designers, as well as fashion features. You could also try foreign and specialist wedding dress magazines for inspiration.

Shops – you usually need an appointment to try on dresses, but you can browse to get an idea of the ranges they carry.

Wedding shows – many designers and retailers attend to wedding shows. The dresses here are often dramatically cut in price – so be prepared to make a quick decision if you see one you like.

What to consider before buying your dress

Although it might feel as though finding the perfect dress is a tough-enough job, actually buying it also involves a lot of thought, time, decisions and, not surprisingly, money!

Before you even think about making that purchase, you need to consider the following:

Budget – how much will you spend?

The average amount spent on a wedding dress is around £750; a high-street store, off-the-peg dress, bought in the sales, can cost considerably less and, of course, a couture dress will cost considerably more. Although some brides strike lucky and find the dress of their dreams at a reduced price, many more overspend the budget in this area. Whenever you set a budget, always factor in 10 per cent for overspends – but then try and stick to this outer limit.

The bride's family traditionally pays for the dress – and for the bridesmaids' dresses. Nowadays, more bridesmaids pay for their own dresses, but this needs to be agreed in advance, and it means that they should have at least some say in their outfits!

Theme – will your dress fit with the rest of your look and day?

The trend for weddings is for their overall design to become ever more coordinated and themed. Although it is by no means a requirement, usually the style of the dress matches the style of the wedding. After all, if you're a minimalist girl at heart, you're likely to regret going for the pink Cinderella outfit when the rest of your wedding is stark black and white. Plus, you'll probably want the bridesmaids to wear similar styles of dress.

Religious considerations

An obvious one, here – some people may be offended if they turn up at, say, a wedding in a cathedral to see the bride in a short, off-the-shoulder number.

Timing – how far in advance do you want to buy it?
Some future brides worry that if they don't start looking the minute they get engaged, they won't find 'The One' in time. Others panic that if they find a dress too soon, they will later find another dress they prefer. These two scenarios do happen, but hardly ever. The main thing to remember is that, unless you are particularly lucky, it will usually take three to five months for your dress to arrive. So, if you have enough time, start looking between six and 12 months in advance of the big day. According to a recent Confetti survey, this is when over 55 per cent of brides start looking.

Partner in crime – whose advice do you want?
It is rare for a bride-to-be to go shopping for her dress alone. So make sure your 'assistant' is available on the day!

Timing – how much time have you allocated to looking for your dress?

Rather like house-hunting, wedding dress-buying is not something you can generally do casually. Even if you love the first dress you see, unless you are seriously busy or allergic to shopping, you'll want to look around further. Don't hope to find the dress in one Saturday – commit to several trips out.

Sizes and samples

The dress you try on in the store is just a sample. Your dress will have to be ordered, so don't worry if the one you're given is covered in make-up and smudges! Sometimes, however, stores do have sample sales – and you may be able to pick up a bargain!

Pictures and photographs

A picture is worth a thousand words – especially when you're trying to communicate to a store assistant the type of dress you want. So make sure you take along some examples of what you're looking for. Don't expect stores to allow you to photograph their dresses, however – this is an issue of copyright (see page 79).

Storage and transport

How are you going to get your pride and joy home, and where will you keep your dress before the big day? Remember, your groom-to-be mustn't see it! There's more about storage later, but remember the short-term option of a duvet cover and some lavender to keep the moths off is just that – short-term.

And afterwards...

What are you planning to do with it afterwards? If you want to dye it and recycle it as an evening gown, check the material will dye effectively.

Checklist for buying a wedding dress

Although this list mostly assumes you will be buying a dress from a shop, it's still useful for buying a second-hand dress or if you're having one made.

- How much is the deposit and when is it due?
- How far before the wedding must you order your dress?
- How far before the wedding can you expect your dress to arrive?
- How many fittings will you need?
- Can you arrange at least one fitting with your bridal lingerie, shoes and other accessories?
- What is the cancellation/postponement policy?
- How much is the deposit and when is it due?
- When is the balance due?
- Is VAT included in the final price?
- Confirm appointments for fittings and collection dates with a written contract.
- Have you insured the dress?

Where to buy your dress

If you're buying a new dress, then you have a remarkable choice of possible suppliers.

The obvious place to look is in specialist bridal stores. According to our survey, 85% of brides say they'll be looking here. To find your nearest bridal stores, check the Confetti supplier directory:
www.confetti.co.uk/confetti_pages/default.asp

Department stores traditionally have dedicated wedding departments. While these normally carry a smaller range of accessories than specialist stores, they are an excellent place to look for dresses. Plus, most people know where their local department store is and are familiar with it, so it's a good place to start.

Recently, high-street stores have begun including wedding and bridesmaids' dresses in their collections. While the range is usually less extensive than those you'll find in other outlets, prices reflect the high-street labels, making this a very affordable option for those on a tight budget.

Buying a once-owned dress

This has never been a more popular or simple option.

The Internet

Many brides sell their once-worn (and sometimes never worn) dresses privately over the Internet. At Confetti, this facility is known as the 'For Sale' message board located at: www.confetti.co.uk/cafe/message_board/sale/topics.asp?id=18 Auction sites can also be a fruitful source.

Charity shops

You may also have seen wedding dresses in the windows of your local charity shops. This is certainly a very inexpensive option, if you are lucky enough to find a size and style to suit you. The charity Oxfam has gone as far as creating five 'bridal boutiques', dedicated to wedding dresses and accessories. As well as not costing the earth, the dresses in these boutiques are sold in a good cause, and also offer the excitement of going to a dress shop – something that may be missing from your local charity shop.

Dress agencies

There are a few dress agencies that specialize in bringing together 'pre-loved' dresses and new owners. You can find these in the Confetti Supplier Directory or the Yellow Pages. Alternatively, try a search on the Internet.

Hiring

There are very few wedding dress hire companies left in the UK, largely because of the high cost of cleaning a wedding dress, which leads to very expensive hire rates. You can find a good list of the remaining hire companies in the Confetti Supplier Directory at: www.confetti.co.uk/confetti_pages/default.asp

Theatre companies and theatrical costumiers often have wedding dresses for hire, however, so it's always worth looking up your nearest company in the Yellow Pages.

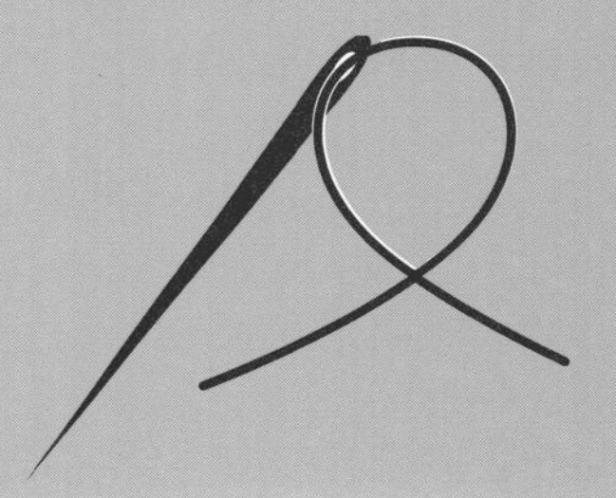

Using a dressmaker

If you are lucky enough to know or find a skilled dressmaker, you have a choice of approaches. You might find a pattern you like, and have her (or him) make it up for you. Alternatively, if you have a very talented dressmaker, you might ask her (or him) to make up a pattern for you from a dress shape you already have.

Some dressmakers ask you to supply your own material; others supply it themselves. In either event, you need to be sure that the material will suit the pattern. Your dressmaker will be able to advise on this.

The most important thing on this subject is that you should be aware that dress designs are under copyright. Taking a picture of a dress you like by a certain designer and asking a dressmaker to copy it is copyright infringement, which is a crime.

Making your own

This is probably best avoided unless you are a very talented and experienced seamstress, or very organized (or preferably both). Weddings are stressful occasions, and sitting up making last-minute changes till one o'clock in the morning every night of the week before your big day will not help. Nor will suddenly realizing you have sewed on a panel back to front or upside down endear your dress to you. You want to love that gown, not remember endless twisted threads or broken needles!

If you do go for making your own, make sure you have enough space to keep the dress and all its material away from dust (or grubby fingers). Allow plenty of time in advance of the wedding, and coopt an assistant to help you with fittings. As with using a dressmaker, copying another designer's dress is illegal – so don't do it!

Couture

A couture dress is a one-off creation, cut and shaped to meet the bride's precise requirements. The design, size and fabrics are all chosen individually for this unique garment.

The length of time required to make a couture piece depends on the style and the date of the wedding. The designing and fitting process consists of a consultation with the bride, during which many measurements are taken, and after which a *toile* (mock-up of the dress) is made. This is then used as a pattern for the real thing.

When you go for your *toile* fitting, you should wear your planned underwear and shoes – it's rather like having a fitting for a dress proper. Now is the time to change anything you aren't keen on – after all, it's only a mock-up and can bear even drastic changes.

Only at this point is the final agreement made on the dress. Then the dress is made in the chosen fabric, followed by the final fittings.

Shopping for your dress

Who to take

Many brides – over 70 per cent, according to a Confetti survey – choose to take their mothers, if possible. However, you know your mother best, and if there's a chance that this particular pairing may cause more rows than harmonious agreements, steer clear. Although this book aims to help make buying your wedding dress as stress-free as possible, it's still best to avoid situations that you know might get a little heated. Whoever you take, make sure it's someone whose taste you trust and who will be honest with you. Also, take someone who is genuinely interested in watching you try on dresses all day – friendships have been tested when brides have felt their shopping partner wasn't showing enough commitment!

When to go

Most stores require an appointment. As trying on dresses can take a long time and a lot of attention from the staff, this is a good idea. When making appointments, remember not to have them too close together, and timetable regular breaks! Try to avoid scheduling appointments for when you have your period or are feeling bloated.

What to wear

In order to gain the full effect, and get the right size, you need to try on dresses wearing the same kind of shoes as those you plan to wear on the day. If at all possible, aim to have roughly the same hairstyle, as many stores will have tiaras and veils for you to try on at the same time. Understandably, you probably won't know what kind of underwear you need until you have chosen your dress style, but if you know you are looking for a clingy or halterneck dress, for instance, make sure you are wearing appropriate undergarments!

What to take

Pad and pen – to note down ideas, thoughts, reminders.
Baby wipes – invaluable for cleaning your hands and generally freshening up.
Camera – once you've put down the deposit, you'll want to remember what Your Dress looks like!
Bottled water – most stores will offer you some but do take your own.

The store assistants

The store staff should be thoroughly knowledgeable and able to give the help or advice you need. It's important that you buy your dress from a shop where you feel comfortable – after all, it's quite a lengthy process from choosing it to taking it home, and you have to feel you can trust the staff. Good store assistants recognize the importance of this purchase and treat every bride and dress as special.

A word about... alcohol

If you are suffering from nerves, or just feel in need of some support, it may be tempting to have a large glass of wine – or something equally fortifying – at lunch while you are shopping. Remember, though, that our most intelligent and considered decisions are not necessarily made while we are a little tipsy, and it's important to keep a clear head. Some bridal stores may offer you a glass of wine. Depending on your tolerance of alcohol, this is fine – as long as you don't visit four stores in a row and have a glass of wine at each!

Fittings

Fittings are opportunities to make alterations to ensure your dress fits perfectly.

Generally speaking, when shopping in a store very few brides will be lucky enough to find the dress of their dreams, in their size and in stock. Often, the dress is ordered in the right size from the designer or manufacturer, and fitted to the bride when it comes into the store. Any alterations will be made after this first fitting, and there will be a second fitting to make sure everything has been done correctly, after which the bride normally takes the dress home.

Most bridal retailers offer these initial fittings as part of their sales service, but they may charge for further fittings or alterations. Some retailers charge for all fittings.

You will definitely need more fittings if you are having a made-to-measure or couture dress, so allow enough time in your wedding preparations for these.

Timeline

12 months before

- Decide your budget and style and colour of gown.
- Research designers and stockists.
- Consult family and friends.

11–8 months before

- Make appointments to try on your favourite dresses.
- Research the most appropriate accessories, underwear and shoes.
- Keep a note of which dresses you like best, and the pros and cons of each.

7–5 months before

- Bring your shoes, headdress, veil, underwear and any other accessories to the first fitting. Make the decision and order your gown.
- Once you have placed an order take a photo of yourself in the dress so you can remember how you look in it.
- Try on different accessories with your dress.
- The second fitting should just be necessary to check everything was done properly. However, if you're losing weight, it might need to be adjusted again. If you're intending to lose weight, its best to get to your target weight before your first fitting to avoid this.

- If you're not happy with the results on your second fitting, schedule another. After all, the purpose of these sessions is to make sure the dress fits properly!
- On your last fitting, bring someone with you so they will know how your gown does up. This will be invaluable for helping you get dressed on the day.

Three weeks before

- Pick up your dress. If the dress is not supplied with a cover, take a cotton duvet to cover it with.
- Plan ahead and find a dry cleaner in advance who specializes in cleaning wedding dresses. Arrange for it to be dropped off after the wedding (preferably while you are on honeymoon!).

One week before

- Try on your dress one last time. Resist the temptation to parade around the house in it unless you are absolutely sure there is no dust, sticky fingers or moulting cats to cause any accidents!

The day before

- Remove the cover from your dress and hang it up to air (where it won't pick up any smells!)
- Check for creases – depending on the material, you may need to steam it.

Wearing and caring for your dress

The general order of getting dressed on the day is as follows:
Underwear
Hair
Make-up

Twenty minutes before you are due to leave:
Dress
Shoes
Veil
Gloves

You will probably need the help of at least one other person to get into (and out of) your dress. Ask your assistant (most probably your chief bridesmaid or your mother) to hold the dress for you to step into, and pull it up over your body. If the dress really needs to go over your head, cover your face with a (preferably silk) scarf to prevent you from smudging your make-up – or worse, getting lippy on the dress.

Your lovely assistant will then need to assist you with doing up zips, laces, hooks and eyes and buttons, depending on your dress's fastenings. If your dress has many hooks or buttons, it's not a bad idea to count them in advance, so your assistant can check them off as she goes. This means you won't discover later on that they haven't all been done up properly.

Then you can be helped into your shoes. Don't try to bend over to do them up, and if you must sit down, don't do so on the back of your gown – remember, this is what everyone sees in the church. Sit on a backless stool or drape the back of your skirt over the back of the chair.

Get your assistant to give you a last lookover before you leave for the ceremony. If possible, take a look at yourself in a full-length mirror, but avoid walking around the house too much in a full skirt – you don't want to sweep it through water on the bathroom floor or the dog's bowl in the kitchen.

Wearing it

Be specially careful getting into your transport to the ceremony venue – you don't want to pick up a smear of engine oil on the way. Make sure your dress is arranged to minimize creases. If you are wearing a veil over your face, you may not want to cover your face until you get to the venue, so you can see what is happening.

You will probably wear your dress in its full glory only for the ceremony itself. After this, the detachable parts or trains of fancier dresses can be bustled, which will aid movement during the day.

Don't try to deal with your dress on your own. Ask for your bridesmaids' help to make sure your skirt is lying properly during photos, and don't attempt to go to the loo on your own. For brides in voluminous skirts, this is a two-person job, and those in ball gowns may have to take their dresses off altogether.

Emergencies

You should give a 'wedding handbag' to your chief bridesmaid to carry for emergencies. What do you need to put in it to keep your outfit in tip top condition during the day?

Spare stockings or tights

If you're one of those people who only has to look at a pair of stockings to ladder them, it's worth carrying spares, just in case the worst happens.

Anti-perspirant

If you're prone to stress sweats, this is a must. If your sleeves are tight-fitting, you might want to get your dressmaker to sew in some perspiration pads, so as to avoid those unsightly underarm damp patches.

Aching feet

After posing for too many photos, pep up tired and swelling feet with a cooling foot spray. These tend to come in fairly large containers, but you can decant a small amount into a handbag-size vaporizer.

Safety pins

These are for just in case the worst happens and a zip goes.

Baby wipes

These will remove most small stains and unsightly smudges that might occur during the day.

Getting undressed

On the happy couple's first night together, few brides can manage the transition from wedding dress to seductive lingerie alone. Usually you will need your new husband's help to undo all those buttons, laces, hooks and eyes. As most husbands are – and rightly so – fairly inexpert at this (and possibly a little tired, too!), allow some time and be patient. Let the dress drop to the floor and then take his hand to step over the skirts.

Many brides like to lay their dress on a clean sheet under the bed for the night. It doesn't matter too much what you do with it, as it is only for one night, but don't wrap it in plastic and don't fold it into sharp creases. It's not a disaster if you simply leave it on the floor for that night!

After the big day

Cleaning and preserving your dress

A word to the wise – a floor-length dress will almost certainly get fairly filthy around the hem during the day. The church or register office will have had a lot of people walking through it, as will your reception venue; you will also have had your pictures taken outside. Yes, you can stand on a clean sheet to prevent any grass stains. Yes, you can demand no one smokes or drinks when talking to you. Yes, you can have the dance floor swept every hour. But… it's probably much better to relax, enjoy the day and get the dress cleaned afterwards!

Find a dry cleaner who specializes in wedding dresses and evening gowns. Alternatively, take a look in Confetti's Supplier Directory or ask other brides on the message boards. Cleaning is pricey – but it needs to be done, whether you are keeping your dress or selling it.

There are companies that sell attractive boxes specially for storing wedding dresses in. The main rules for storage are: keep your dress out of sunlight, don't wrap it in plastic, use acid-free paper, don't squash it, use a padded hanger and don't allow other items to snag it.

Customizing or selling your dress

You may want to transform your dress into one you can wear again. If so, take advice from the people from whom you originally purchased it.

Dyeing is a popular option, but this really requires the advice and services of a professional. Find one in your area in the Confetti Supplier Directory.

If you want to sell your dress, you can do this either privately or through a dress agency. A private sale is easy and cheap through the Internet – most sites charge a small commission (although Confetti is free). Discuss the dress agency's terms with them carefully, and if they want to keep your dress on their premises, make sure you have a contract to cover the risk of it being damaged before it is sold.

Some bridal stores may buy your dress back from you after you have worn it, and then sell it as once-worn. Beware as the offer may not be as good as it sounds: it may make it a very expensive dress to wear once and then have little to show for it.

Bridesmaids' dresses

You may think that choosing a wedding dress is quite a tricky job. But once you begin looking for bridesmaids' gowns, you may feel that selecting a bridal gown was the easy part!

Whoever your bridesmaids are, there obviously has to be some kind of compromise reached between your ideas and what each of them feels like wearing. Bear in mind that these are close friends and relatives you are picking outfits for, not Barbie. Think about their individual personalities and tastes, and don't expect bridesmaids to wear something you yourself wouldn't be comfortable in.

The matter of who is paying for the dresses moves the boundaries a little. If you are stumping up the readies, bridesmaids may be pleased to have a dress they can wear again, but shouldn't necessarily expect it. However, if you are asking them to shell out, you should expect to decide on a dress that your attendants can wear again. Avoiding outré colours and patterns is, therefore, a must. Nobody is suggesting that you should kit out your bridesmaids in jumpers and jeans, but if you choose something a tiny bit practical, your bridesmaids will love you for it, and that precious compromise may be reached a little sooner.

Bridesmaids' dress styles

As the bride, you have the right to point out that bridesmaids should resist the temptation to impose their own style on your wedding. Your Gothic-style younger sister doesn't absolutely have to have a black dress just because that's the only thing she'd choose.

A good practical solution is to opt for separates, rather than one-piece dresses – even if they'll never wear that fuchsia bodice again, they might wear the grey silk skirt (or vice versa).

Another complication is that few brides are lucky enough to have bridesmaids who all have the same type of skin, hair tone and body shape. However, if you have your heart set on a particular colour theme, you could suggest that each bridesmaid chooses a style of dress most suitable for her within that colour range. This is a very popular approach in America, and many US designers are now bringing their ranges over here: check the bridesmaids section of the Confetti dress database for inspiration.

Alternatively, you can ask all your bridesmaids to wear the same style and fabric, but let them choose the colour. This can look really stunning.

Choosing a black tie dress code is another way to solve the bridesmaids issue. Bridesmaids in evening dress look great at urban, evening, register office and large formal weddings. Your bridesmaids will love you for this too, because every woman can use another dress for those occasions when she needs to get dressed up and suddenly realizes she has nothing to wear.

If you have a number of bridesmaids, it's difficult to get everyone together for shopping trips. So do as much advance research as you possibly can in order to minimize the organization involved! Bridesmaids' outfits can usually be found in all the same outlets as bridal wear.

The pregnant bridesmaid

One of the subjects on which Confetti's agony aunt receives most mail from panicking brides is the problem of the bridesmaid who announces she is pregnant. Although this is a tricky situation, as no one can know with any certainty what size the bridesmaid will be on the day, it is by no means insurmountable. Consider these options:

Buy your bridesmaids' outfits from department stores and retailers with large stock lines and a wide range of sizes. This way you can leave it to the last possible moment to find the right size – and you don't have to wait for delivery.

Have your bridesmaids' outfits made by a seamstress. This way the pregnant bridesmaid can have her dress made last, and you get the chance to check the style and quality of the dresses for the other bridesmaids.

Outfits for little attendants

The littlest bridesmaids are often known as flower girls. Most flower girls carry a small bouquet or basket of either flowers or petals to sprinkle as they walk down the aisle. They may wear a different outfit from other bridesmaids: some brides like to dress them in little flower fairy costumes (and this is almost sure to be a hit with the girls themselves!). A new trend in America – decide for yourself whether or not it should cross the pond – is for the flower girl to dress as a mini-bride in white and a veil!

Whatever outfit you decide upon, remember that kids grow at an alarming rate. Don't buy the outfit too far in advance, or you'll be looking for another child to fit into it! Flower girl accessories depend upon the dress, but may include a tiara, a wreath of flowers or decorative hairclips. They also depend to a degree on what the child will consent to wear, so bear this in mind.

Matron (or maid) of honour

You may want your matron of honour to stand out from the rest of the bridesmaids in a different colour or style of dress. Alternatively, she could wear a wrap or gloves.

Best women

If you (rather than the groom) are having a best woman, then she may want to select a smart suit (skirt or trousers) and a hat for her outfit. To ensure people realize that she is part of the wedding party and not simply a guest, the outfit could be in one of the themed 'wedding colours'.

Lady ushers

Ushers are generally male and wear the same as the rest of the wedding party. But, if you are having female ushers, and they aren't wearing morning suits with the male ushers, make sure they have corsages to help them stand out.

Accessories

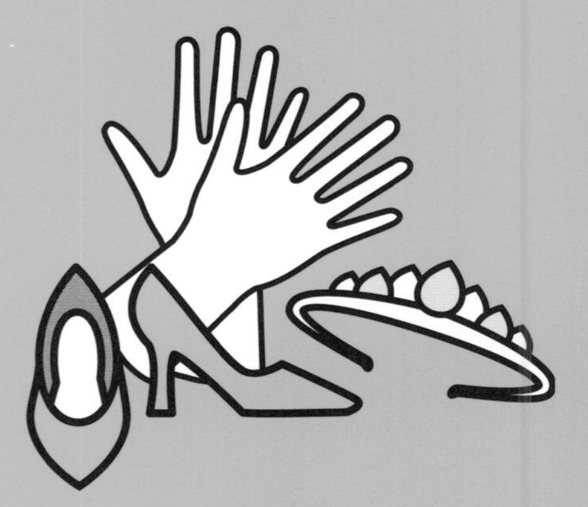

The dress is, of course, not just a dress.

It's actually just one part of an entire look created by a combination of elements, including the headdress (feathers? jewels? flowers?), veil (long? short? down or up?), gloves (how do you get the darn ring on?), shoes (high? low? more than one pair?), cover-up (cloak? jacket? wrap?) and, of course, underwear.

These items need careful consideration in their own right (and, of course, careful budgeting!). But they are all part of the custom and tradition of getting married, and consequently, each has a value beyond what you actually pay for it. This is also a great opportunity to include 'something borrowed' – what about trying Mum's veil? Or Gran's tiara?

Once you've assembled this outfit, you'll be guarding it with your life. But there's one thing you can't control – the weather. So don't forget your wedding umbrella! See www.confetti.co.uk/shopping/default.asp for shopping advice and ideas.

Headdresses

Modern western headdresses vary greatly in style. You can pick up an inexpensive 'crown' from any accessory shop, or get a made-to-order tiara sculpted to perfection – a work of art in itself.

Whether you fancy doing the royalty thing and crowning yourself with a diamanté-studded effort, or would rather go for a more delicate, flower-based hairband, there are numerous ways of fixing a veil or pinning back hair. You just need to know where to start looking.

Where to start

A good place to start is at your hair salon. Pop in for a consultation (you'll probably be doing this anyway, to discuss your hair style) and ask to flick through some hair magazines, or see if they keep an album of different ways to wear tiaras and flowers. Don't forget the detail around the back of your head is as important as the front view because for most of the ceremony you will have your back to your guests.

If your hair is very fine, it may not hold a heavy tiara. Wash it the day before the wedding to give it more chance of holding a headpiece, and give your hairdresser ample time to secure it in place. If you're feeling brave, branch out from beads and sequins, and adorn your headdress with something more daring. Try kingfisher feathers, for instance, as woven into hair pieces by the ancient Chinese. Finally, when visiting the dress shop for your final fitting, remember to take your headdress along with you.

Guide to headdress styles

Tiara – for the regal touch.
Band – a simple headband worn towards the front of the head.
Bun – a circular band encircling a bun hair style.
Crown – a romantic tiara style adorned with stones or sequins.
Snood – a net fitted over the back of the head, bun-style.
Juliet cap – *à la* 'Romeo and…', a round cap sitting closely on top of the head.
Wreath – a band of flowers or foliage worn towards the front of the head.

Gloves

It's not essential for a bride to wear gloves on her big day, but, when chosen with care, they can complement an outfit beautifully, and they make a popular addition to the finished effect of dress, veil and tiara.

Handy history

The Victorians were the first great glove-wearers. They would wear them at all kinds of occasions, according to their status – the better off you were, the more likely it was that you would possess a selection to wear whenever you were out of doors or at any social function. The fashion for wearing gloves at weddings, formal parties and dances was revived in the 1930s and 1940s.

Why wear gloves?

These days gloves are worn at many weddings as a fashion statement, though they do have other more practical uses. They protect a wedding dress from any natural oils on a bride's fingers, or from snagged fingernails, and they can help keep her warm during a winter ceremony. Well, a bit warmer – after all, we're not talking woolly mitts here! Bridal gloves are usually slender satin confections, designed to fit the bride's arm length.

Common glove styles

Fingerless – think 1980s rock chick. Handy for ring-fitting and canapé-munching, but could be chilly in winter.
Gauntlet – this arm-length glove goes right down to the wrist, but doesn't cover the hand.
Elbow – ends just above the elbow.
Opera – similar to elbow style, but reaching to the upper arm.
Wrist – 'ordinary' gloves, covering the hand only.

When to wear them

Generally, you can wear gloves for most of the day (except while eating), and especially during evening events. You can remove them just before the ring-giving part of the ceremony and pass them to your maid-of-honour to hold, then replace them after the service or during the signing of the register. The whole process can be a bit fiddly, so get some practice in before your wedding day. If you plan to walk back down the aisle without your gloves, make sure you remove both in order to avoid looking lopsided! Alternatively, make a small cut down the underside of your glove's ring finger or split the seam, so that you can slip your finger out for the exchanging of rings, and back in again afterwards. Some gloves come ready split for this purpose.

Choosing and fitting gloves

There's more to the phrase 'fits like a glove' than you might think! In fact, it's important to get yourself properly measured when buying a pair – head for your nearest department store or buy them from the same place as your wedding dress.

Tips for glove fittings

- Gloves are measured from your middle fingertip.
- The shorter the bride the shorter the glove should be.
- Pick gloves that complement your dress, rather than draw attention away from it.
- Gloves come in all sorts of different fabrics – mesh and cotton have both been popular in recent years.
- Check out vintage clothes shops or costumiers for antique examples, but be sure to choose a style that suits your dress.
- Look for gloves that unbutton at the wrist – these will come in handy during ring-giving.
- If you've found the style you want but not the colour, buy plain gloves and dye them to match your dress (but check the label first to make sure this won't damage the gloves).
- If you have very muscular arms, it is wise to steer clear of gloves altogether.
- Wearing a long-sleeved dress? You probably won't need gloves at all.

Veils

Veils are as old as weddings. The Romans used them to symbolize the flame of Vesta, goddess of the home and provider of life. Some say they were used centuries ago to ward off any evil spirits that might surround a bride as she approached her marriage. Others claim they are a vestige of the ancient tradition of the carrying-off of a bride by the groom, during which he would throw a blanket over her to make the task more manageable.

Common veil styles

Veils are split into categories according to length, from shoulder-through to cathedral-length, the longest and most formal. Delicate creations may be fashioned from tulle or lace, and they are often incorporated into hats or headdresses.

Shoulder – a short piece covering the head and neck.

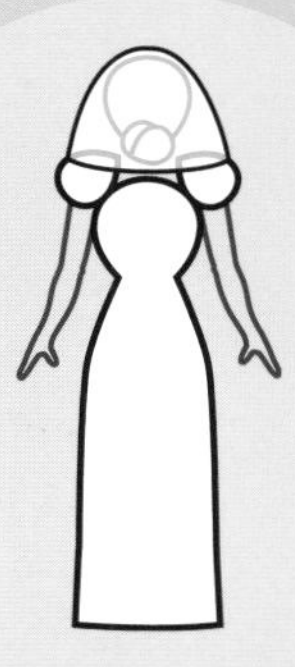

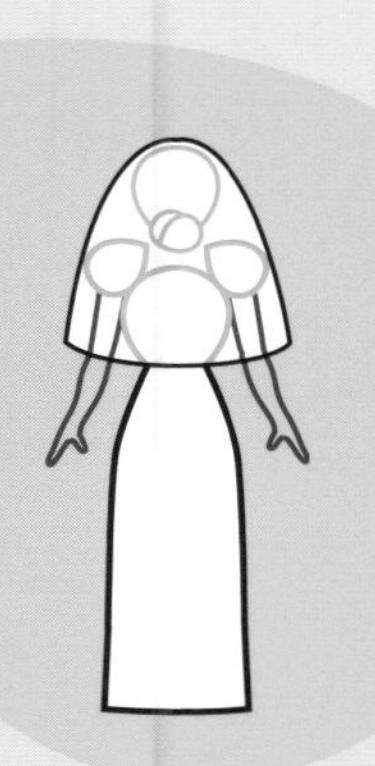

Elbow – falls halfway down the arms.

Fingertip – just as it says, reaches down to cover the hands.

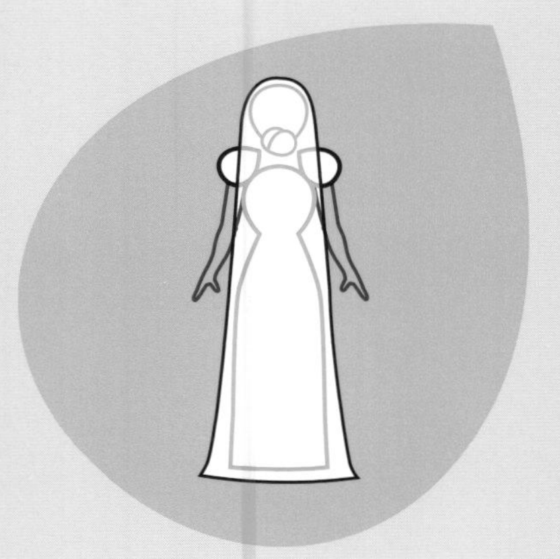

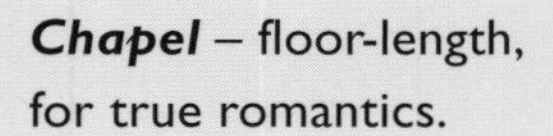

Chapel – floor-length, for true romantics.

Cathedral – the real thing! A long, flowing, fairytale headpiece designed to trail behind you as you walk. Will require bridesmaids!

Practicalities

These days, veils usually serve to add the finishing touch to a gown. They can also help a bride meet her 'something old/new/borrowed/blue' quota, depending on taste and family heirlooms.

When choosing a veil, there are a few considerations to bear in mind. If the dress is detailed, keep the veil simple. A long veil can help deflect attention from a wide waist, but make sure it doesn't also distract from any bows or details down the back of the dress. If you really want to go for it with your veil, and you're handy with the glue and sequins, then buy a simple veil and go crazy with adornments.

When it comes to wearing your veil, let your hairdresser know well in advance what kind of veil you plan, so it can be made as secure as possible. If your veil covers your face, keep it at bust height so that it doesn't cover your flowers.

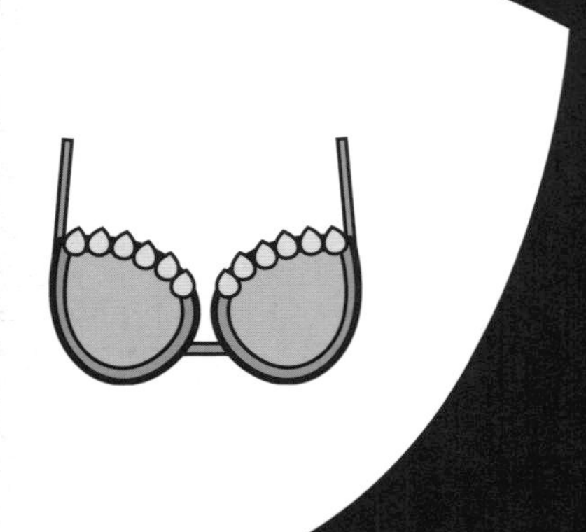

Bridal underwear

If you've learnt one thing from this book, it's probably that the best advice is to try on your dress with the underwear you plan to wear on the day. But with so many kinds, what, exactly, is what and which are suitable for which dress style?

Bra

Ah, the bra. Where would we be without it. Nowadays, there is a style to go with every type of wedding dress, be it strapless, backless, frontless, halterneck, underwired, reducing or push-up. The key here is to find a bra that you are comfortable in. Persistent itching or readjusting will not add to the pleasure of your day. If you are wearing a heavily corseted dress, you may not require a bra, but in most cases you will.

Bustier

A bustier is akin to a bra that reaches down to the waist. It is often boned and offers the added benefit of holding you in down the torso. This is an absolutely ideal way to avoid noticeable bra lines across your back if you're wearing a sheer or tight bodice, and a blessing for pulling tummies in just that little bit more.

Corset

The defining aspect of a corset is that it has laces that can be pulled tightly to define your figure. Corsets are mostly strapless, and as well as being very popular wedding dress foundation garments, they are also a favourite shape for the top half of a ball gown or a fishtail dress composed of separates.

Basque

A basque incorporates a bra, body control and suspenders all in one, and is a simple way of dealing with a lot of underwear! It's also a sexy outfit to wear under a demure ball gown.

Suspenders

Suspenders and stockings still top the charts for bridal legs, ahead of tights or bare legs. Stockings come in two forms: hold-ups and clip-ons. The latter are attached to a suspender belt, which coordinates with your other underwear.

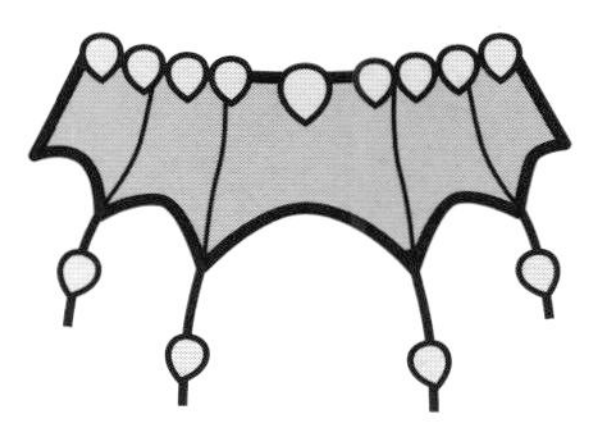

Girdle

The girdle that was familiar to most people's grandmothers has been reborn today in the form of stomach-and-thigh control pants. Looking rather like cycling shorts, these give a clean line over the stomach, bottom and thighs, and are therefore great for wearing under clinging dresses.

Hooped petticoat

Most ball gown dresses require a hooped petticoat underneath to keep the skirts fully extended and circular. You will usually be able to purchase one at the same time as you buy your dress.

Garter

Don't forget your garter! At American weddings, when the bride throws her bouquet to the ladies, the groom removes her garter and throws it to the men!

A word about tights and stockings

If you wear these with open-toe shoes, make sure you choose either 'sandal' tights with no seam across the toe, or open-toe tights and stockings, which are now available at most lingerie outlets.

Cloaks, jackets, wraps and stoles

Covering bare arms is a must in winter, and a stylish jacket can look amazing with the right dress. A sophisticated jacket with a high collar and flared bell sleeves will make a statement and keep you warm for those outdoor photos. Some dress styles come with little bolero jackets as part of the design.

Alternatively, go for a fake fur coat or hooded cloak in luxuriously warm, sensuous velvet. If it's the middle of summer and you just like the thought of having a coat to finish off your look, a full-length, floaty coat or long wrap in a transparent or glittery material makes a very popular choice. Few of these will go with a full skirt, but they can really complement a straight dress.

Many stores stock a great range of wraps and stoles in a variety of silks, cashmeres, satins and velvets, both plain and embroidered. If you want your accessories to be kind to the budget, check out your usual shopping haunts, as well as the bridal stores.

If you are wearing a coat, jacket or wrap, it's usual to take it off during the ceremony. If it's just too cold, then by all means keep it on, but remember the guests will see only your back for much of the time.

Things you need to know about your wedding shoes!

Wear open-toe sandals with bare feet or 'sandal' tights

There's nothing more off-putting than a thick nylon seam across the toes – unless it's an unpedicured set of tootsies. Make sure nails are neat, trimmed and painted – this could be a good place for your 'something blue'!

Don't wear a heel more than 3cm (1in) higher than you usually wear

Apart from the fact that you will be on your feet practically all day, wearing a higher heel than you're accustomed to will compress your calf muscles and make your legs ache, as well as your feet. And, remember, you might be expected to dance the night away!

Don't wear leather with a dress

Unless they have very thin little straps, leather shoes just look too clumpy with most dresses and evening suits. Fabric – silk or satin – shoes are much more appropriate, as are shiny or diamanté finishes.

Do feel free to have two pairs of shoes

If you want to have one pair for walking down the aisle and having your photos taken, and another for the reception, go ahead! Many brides nowadays change into more comfortable shoes – or even trainers – for the reception.

Do take your shoes to your dress fitting

Once you've decided on your dress style and colour, you can safely purchase your shoes. Just as it makes sense to try on your dress with the appropriate lingerie, so you should wear the right shoes to check the length. You don't want to discover that you've had your dress made just too short or too long, so you either trip over it or show an unflattering amount of ankle.

Do make sure you can walk in them

First, ensure your shoes are not going to slip off with every second step, or need constant adjusting. If you aren't comfortable in them, don't wear them – it will show. Second, check they don't make any weird sounds when you walk. You don't want to make annoying clicking or slopping noises all the way down the aisle!

Shoes should complete, not dominate, your outfit

This is a tricky one for those of us who've never minded what old jeans we are wearing as long as we've had a fabulous pair of boots on the end of our legs. But however much you love shoes and feel lukewarm about dresses, people will probably notice the latter before the former. So try not to accessorize a Vera Wang sheath dress with a pair of Vivienne Westwood royal blue ribbon-tie platform shoes.

Do be careful with delicate dresses and beaded shoes

That beautiful decoration on the toes of your shoes shouldn't be a trap for the delicate lace on the hem of your dress. Make sure they won't catch on each other – at best, it will annoy you; at worst, it will trip you up!

Do wear them in

You don't want to get blisters, find out you can't walk in them or, worse, slip over because the soles are too shiny. Pull a pair of old socks over your shoes while wearing them around the house. If the soles are slippery, rough them up a bit using a fork (but only after you've definitely decided you don't need to take them back!).

Most fabric shoes can be dyed

If you can't find the exact colour you want, don't despair... many companies offer a bespoke dyeing service. Look for one near you online in Confetti's Supplier Directory.

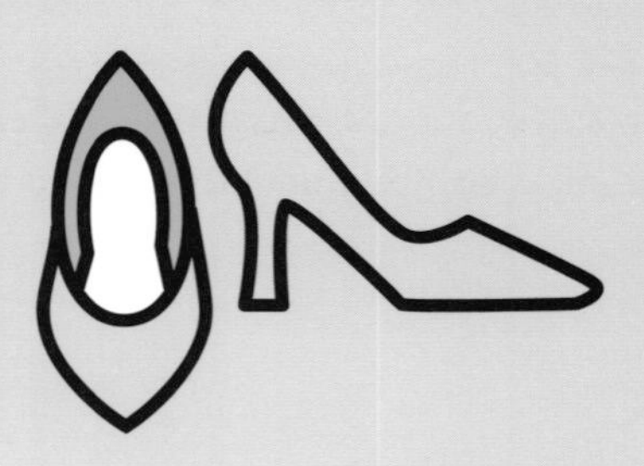

And finally... the going-away outfit

Traditionally, the happy couple left the reception before their guests and changed into 'going-away outfits' to speed off to their honeymoon. Nowadays, things are a little different. You've spent more than you should have on the dress of your dreams. You love it, and you don't want to take it off! Do you have to wear a going-away outfit? Well no, of course not. Many brides and grooms are practically the last couple off the dance floor anyway, so there's often not much point! Most brides don't take off their dress until they get to their first-night hotel.

Glossary

In your search for the perfect dress, you may sometimes wonder exactly what everyone's talking about! Here's a guide to some of the bridal wear terminology you may come across on your quest:

A-line So-called because this dress shape looks like the letter A! Basically, an A-line dress hugs the body at the shoulders and then flares gently outwards.

apron Extra material on a skirt that falls rather like a kitchen apron and has the effect of making the skirt look fuller.

ballerina A wide skirt that reaches to just above the ankles.

ballet veil A veil that reaches the ankles.

ball gown A wide skirt that flares out from a narrow waist and reaches at least to the ankles. A ball gown dress often has a fitted bodice.

band A neckline with a high collar, giving a choker-like effect.

basque A long, tight-fitting bodice that finishes in a V-shape at the front of the dress. Also a type of corset.

bias cut Material cut at a 45-degree angle across the length and width of the fabric, giving a very flattering effect.

bodice Upper part of a dress.

bustle Material gathered at the back of the skirt to make the bottom look more shapely.

cap sleeves Small, tight sleeves, slightly wider at the top, that only just cover the shoulder.

classic A dress with a timeless quality and clean lines.

column/straight A long, straight dress.

contemporary/modern A dress with clean, straight, uncluttered lines.

corset A corset-style bodice that is strapless, fitted, boned and often laced or snap-fastened.

décolletage/décolleté A low-cut neckline.

draped Loose, soft material attached to a garment, usually a skirt.

dropped waist A waistline with a seam that falls a few inches below the natural waist.

elbow gloves Gloves that reach up to the elbow.

empire line A dress with a high waistline and a seam just under the bust.

fishtail A figure-hugging dress in which the skirt fits tightly to the knee before flaring out at the bottom.

flounced A skirt with a ruffle at the bottom, or with lots of layers.

garter A traditional part of bridal underwear, comprising a prettily decorated piece of elastic that goes on the top of the stocking.

gauntlet glove A long glove that reaches down to the wrist but does not cover the hand.

historical design A design which incorporates elements of dresses from different periods, for example 1920s, Edwardian, 1950s, medieval. Can resemble period costume. Perfect for themed weddings.

jewel A neckline that circles the natural neckline.

Juliet cap A small hat that sits on the back of the head.

keyhole yoke A high-necked dress with cut-aways near the bust or throat.

medieval/gothic A dress that incorporates elements of medieval costume, possibly with Celtic embroidery or a floaty veil.

mermaid A figure-hugging dress that flares out at the bottom.

off-the-shoulder A neckline that lies just over the top of the bust, leaving the shoulders uncovered.

opera gloves Gloves that reach up to the upper arm.

peplum A flap of material at the waist of a dress that is attached to create the impression of an hourglass figure.

pillbox A high, small, brimless hat.

portrait An off-the-shoulder neckline.

princess-line A dress that fits tightly at the top, then flares out gently from a seamless waist, also called A-line.

romantic A big, floaty, dreamy dress.

ruched A style with regularly spaced gathers of material, usually on a skirt.

samples Dresses kept in bridal wear shops from which orders are taken.

sheath A straight, body-hugging dress with no waist.

shoestring/spaghetti straps Very thin straps attached to bodice.

shrug Short, round-edged, non-fastening jacket.

slip dress A version of the column/straight dress style.

three-quarter-sleeve Sleeves which reach just below the elbow.

tiara Jewelled headdress to which a veil can be attached.

tiered A skirt made up of layers of increasing lengths.

Victorian Dress that incorporates elements of Victorian costume. Often a more formal style, this could be based on a Victorian ball gown with a straight front and train, or could be more frilly.

waltz veil A veil that reaches the floor.

wrist gloves Gloves that reach to the wrist.

Confetti.co.uk is the UK's leading wedding and special occasion website, helping more than 400,000 brides, grooms and guests every month.

Confetti.co.uk is packed full of ideas and advice to help organize every stage of your wedding. At Confetti, you can choose from hundreds of beautiful wedding dresses; investigate our list of more than 3,000 wedding and reception venues; plan your wedding; chat to other brides about their experiences and ask for advice from Aunt Betti, our agony aunt. If your guests are online, too, we will even help you set up a wedding website to share details and photos with your family and friends.

Our extensive online content on every aspect of weddings and special occasions is now complemented by our range of books covering every aspect of planning a wedding, for everyone involved. Titles include the complete *Wedding Planner*; *Getting Married Abroad*; *Wedding Readings & Vows*; *The Bride's Wedding*; *The Bridesmaid's Wedding*; *The Groom's Wedding*; *The Father of the Bride's Wedding*; *Men at Weddings*; *Your Daughter's Wedding*; *Wedding & Special Occasion Stationery* and *The Wedding Book of Calm*.

Confetti also offer:
Wedding & special occasion stationery – our stunning ranges include all the pieces you will need for all occasions, including christenings, namings, anniversaries and birthday parties.
Wedding & party products – stocking everything you need from streamers to candles to cameras to cards to flowers to fireworks and, of course, confetti!

To find out more or to order your confetti gift book, party brochure or wedding stationery brochure, visit: www.confetti.co.uk; call: 0870 840 6060; email: info@confetti.co.uk
visit: Confetti, 80 Tottenham Court Road, London W1T 4TE
or Confetti, The Light, The Headrow, Leeds LS1 8TL